RULES OF THE GAME

PICTURE
&
WORD GAMES

D0040236

Crown Publishers, Inc.
One Park Avenue
New York, N.Y. 10016

An Instant Thumb Indexed Product

MANUFACTURED BY
SPINDEX CORPORATION
47-55 37th St., L.I.C., N.Y. 11101
Patent #3,877,729   Made in U.S.A.

SPINDEX REORDER NO. 2105

INTRODUCTION

No matter what the language, people all over the world love picture and word games. The same games can appear in different countries in a variety of forms; human invention modifies existing games and devises new ones. Here, for the first time, is a fully illustrated reference book that descirbes with ease and accuracy many picture and word games that are played throughout the world. Rules and techniques are included here for the beginner, novice, or expert. With a clear text and exact illustrations, RULES OF THE GAME — *Picture & Word Games* provides an easy-to-grasp guide for everyone. It is in fact a major reference book of how to play.

Picture Dominoes

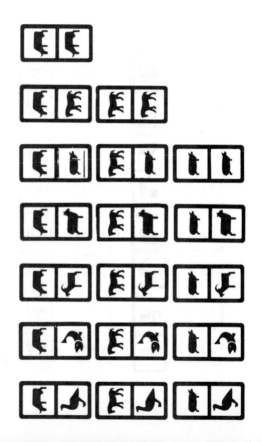

PICTURE DOMINOES

Dominoes with pictures are very popular with young children and can be easily bought or made.

A typical set contains 28 brightly colored dominoes with combinations of seven different pictures. They are usually made of wood or heavy card.

All the dominoes are shared out among the players, who should keep the pictures hidden from the other players. One player starts by placing one domino face upward on the table. Players then take turns at adding a matching domino. If a player doesn't have a matching domino he misses his turn.

The winner is the first player to add all his dominoes to the row on the table.

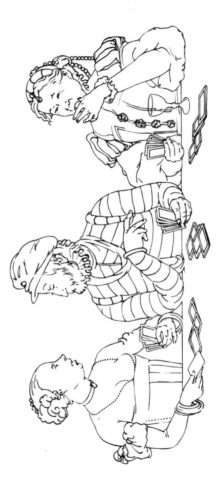

Tarot card games

The exact origins of tarot cards are not known, but it is probable that they have been used since medieval times both as a means of foretelling the future and for playing card games. Many different tarot games are played today, often using a mixed deck of tarot and standard playing cards.

AUSTRIAN TAROCK
This is a popular 54-card tarot game played in many parts of Europe. It is played with a mixed deck of numbered tarot cards and standard playing cards.

Players It is a game for three people (**a**), but can be adapted for four players.

The player to the left of the dealer is called forehand, the next middlehand, and the dealer himself, endhand. (If four players take part (**b**), the dealer does not receive cards, but he may share in the payments for that hand. The third player is then called endhand.)

Trump cards

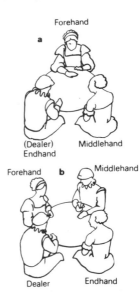

Forehand

a

(Dealer)
Endhand   Middlehand

Forehand   **b**   Middlehand

Dealer   Endhand

The deck comprises:
a) 32 cards divided equally into four suits—hearts, diamonds, spades, and clubs. Four of the eight cards in each suit are court cards: king, queen, knight, and jack. Cards in the red suits rank: k (high),q,kt,j,a,2,3,4 (low). Cards in the black suits rank: k (high),q,kt,j,10,9,8,7 (low).
b) 22 trump cards numbered XXII (high) through I (low). Number XXII is called the joker or "skus;" number XXI "mond;" and number I "pagat."
The trump cards are sometimes illustrated as well as bearing a number.

The objective is to make a winning bid and to score points in melds and tricks.
Deal The dealer gives eight face-down cards at a time to each player, including himself. He then deals a face-down "widow" of six cards to the center of the table, before dealing a further batch of eight cards to each player.
(Should any player not have received a trump card, he must immediately show his cards, and a redeal takes place after the cards have been thoroughly shuffled.)

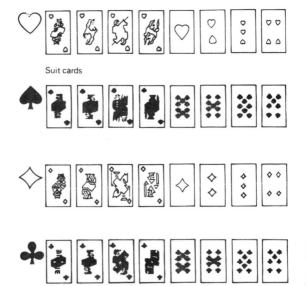

Suit cards

Bidding is in a clockwise direction, beginning with forehand. Players may either bid or pass. If all the players pass, the deal moves one player to the left without a score.

There are two permissible bids: a threesome (worth 50 points) and a solo (worth 100 points). The solo bid overcalls the threesome, so that if forehand opens with a solo bid, there can be no further bidding.

Threesome When the winning bid is threesome, the bidder takes up the top three cards of the widow. If these are not to his liking, he puts them face up on the table and takes the remaining three cards of the widow.

He may either incorporate these three cards into his

Melds

hand (in which case the game counts double); or he may reject them face up and take up the exposed first three cards of the widow (in which case the game counts triple).

Whichever cards he chooses, he then discards any three cards, except kings, from his hand. His discards are put face down on the table but if they include a trump this must be declared.

At the end of play, the discards belong to the winning bidder and the rejected cards of the widow to his two opponents (see the section on trick scores).

After choosing his widow cards, the bidder must choose to play either:

a) game—in which case he must try to win 36 or more points in play; or

b) consolation—in which case he must try to win 35 or fewer points.

Solo When solo is the winning bid, the widow remains unexposed. At the end of play it goes to the bidder's opponents, who, in both solo and threesome, play in partnership against him.

Melds are declared after the bidding and the discarding, if any.

Possible melds are:
a) joker, mond, and pagat;
b) four kings.

Each meld scores 50 in threesome and 100 in solo. (see scoring).

| 5 points | 5 points | 5 points | 5 points |

| 4 points | 3 points | 3 points |

Play After the bidding, forehand leads with any card he likes. The other players must either follow suit or, if this is impossible, trump. If a player can neither follow suit nor trump he may play any card he likes.

The highest trump, or the highest card of the suit led if there are no trumps, takes the trick. The winner of each trick leads to the next trick.

Points in play depend on the combination of "point" cards and "nulls" in each trick. Point cards and their point values are as follows:

a) joker (XXII), mond (XXI), pagat (I), and kings, five points each;

b) queens, four points each; and

c) knights and jacks, three points each.

Nulls are the other 35 cards and have no point values. Each trick counts points as follows:

a) one point for three nulls;

b) the value of the point card for one point card and two nulls;

c) the sum of the point cards minus one, for two point cards and one null; and

d) the sum of the point cards minus two, for three point cards.

The bidder also scores for his discards, if any, and the opponents for the widow. The bidder fulfills his bid if either:

he chose solo or game and makes 36 or more trick points; or he chose consolation and makes 35 or fewer trick points.

Scoring At solo or game a successful bidder scores double the number of trick points he made over 35, plus

50 for threesome and 100 for solo.

If he played consolation, his score would be double the difference between 35 and his actual trick points, plus 50 for threesome.

For example, if he took 24 trick points, his score would be $(35 - 24) \times 2 + 50 = 72$.

If the bidder fails to make his bid, each of his opponents scores the value of the bid plus twice the number of points the opponent has scored over 35.

Each player then scores for any melds he has made.

Pagat Any player who wins the last trick with the pagat receives a bonus of 50 in threesome, and 100 in solo.

Before play opens the bidder may declare "Ultimo," signifying his intention of taking the last trick with the pagat.

If he does so and succeeds, he gains a bonus of twice the value of the game.

If he fails, he loses that same amount. If he has to play the pagat earlier in the game and loses it, he may score 5 points for it if he takes the last trick. He does not score if he played the pagat unnecessarily.

If the bidder declares ultimo, an opponent may declare "Contra-ultimo," signifying that he intends to win the bidder's pagat.

If he does so and succeeds, each opponent wins a bonus of 200 in threesome, and 400 in solo.

If he fails, the same bonus goes to the bidder.

Trick scores

1 point

7 points

5 points

9 points

Batons

Cups

Swords

  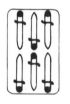 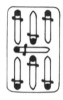

 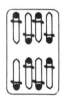

Coins

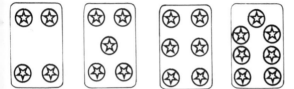

The fool

The juggler

The high priestess

The empress

The emperor

The pope

The lovers

The chariot

Strength

The hermit

The wheel
of fortune

Justice

Death

The hanging man

Temperance

The devil

The star

The tower

The moon

The sun

The world

The day of judgment

TAROCCO

Tarocco is a tarot game played with the traditional 78-card tarot deck that is also used for fortune telling.

Players The game is for three players. Play is in a counterclockwise direction: the player to the dealer's right is called forehand, the second player middlehand, and the dealer endhand.

The deck comprises:
a) 22 cards that function as a trump suit;
b) 56 cards in four suits of 14 cards each: batons, cups, swords, and coins.

The trump cards rank from XXI (high) to I (low). (The fool, when ranked, ranks below the I.)

The suit cards rank k(high), q,kt(knight),j,10,etc.

Deal Players draw cards for the right to deal; lowest card deals first. The deal passes one player to the right for each new hand.

Each player is dealt 24 cards, one at a time and face down. The remaining six cards are added to the dealer's hand.

The trump cards are:
the fool (the only one of the 22 cards that is not numbered), the juggler (I), the high priestess (II), the empress (III), the emperor (IV), the pope (V), the lovers (VI), the chariot (VII), strength (VIII), the hermit (IX), the wheel of fortune (X), justice (XI), the hanging man (XII), death (XIII), temperance (XIV), the devil (XV), the tower (XVI), the star (XVII), the moon (XVIII), the sun (XIX), the day of judgment (XX), and the world (XXI).

The world, the juggler, and the fool are called "honor" cards.

The objective is to score the maximum number of points by taking certain cards in tricks.

Buying cards takes place as soon as the deck has been dealt.

It is an optional procedure and has many variations, but usually a player wanting a particular card may announce this and buy it from the player who holds it (assuming he is willing to part with it) by "paying" ten points ie ten points are deducted from the buyer's score and added to the seller's score.

Play The dealer discards face down any six cards except honors and kings.

He then leads to the first trick by putting out face up any card of his choice. Play then proceeds in a counterclockwise direction. If the lead is in batons, cups, swords, or coins the players must play a card of the same suit but of any value. If he cannot follow suit, he must play a trump card; if this is not possible he may play a card of any suit.

If the lead is a trump card, a player must follow with another trump card—usually a rule is applied that it should also be of a higher value; if this is not possible he may play a card of any suit.

The winner of a trick leads to the next trick.

Scoring in tricks If accompanied by a low-value card (ace through 10) certain cards score as follows:
a) the world (XXI), the juggler (I), the fool, five points each;
b) kings, five points each;
c) queens, four points each;
d) knights, two points each.

The dealer also scores as above for his discards.

The fool A player holding the fool may, during any trick except the last, show it instead of playing a card. The trick is then contested between his two opponents only, and the fool is placed with any tricks the player may have taken. In the last trick, the fool counts as the lowest ranking trump card and is played normally.

The juggler If a player wins the last trick with a juggler, he scores ten points. If he plays the juggler to the last trick and loses, he forfeits ten points.

Bonus points A player with 15 trumps in his hand must declare them before play begins, and earns a bonus of ten points.

A player who wins all tricks receives a bonus of 20 points.

The winner is the player with the highest score at the end of three hands.

Each loser pays the difference between his and the winner's score, according to a points or money scale agreed on by the players before the game.

Japanese flower card games

Japanese flower cards—or "hanafuda" cards—grew from the meeting between Western playing cards and ancient Japanese painted seashell games. Once a cult in court life, hanafuda games spread to the geisha houses and then throughout Japanese society. Cards can be bought in Western countries.

The cards Hanafuda cards are only $2\frac{1}{8}$ in high by $1\frac{1}{4}$ in wide. They are much thicker than Western playing cards. Because of this the Japanese play onto cushions, on which the cards slide less easily. The deck consists of 48 cards. These are divided into 12 suits of four cards each. Each suit represents one of the 12 months of the year. Each card shows a tree or plant, usually one that the Japanese associate with that card's month. Many of the cards show other objects as well.

Most decks also have an additional blank card, which can be used to replace a lost or damaged card.

Card values Each hanafuda card has a point value. These values range from one through 20 points, and there is a distribution within each suit. The standard distribution is one 10 point card, one 5 point card, and two 1 point cards. There are, however, several suits with other distributions.

Usually, in each suit:
a) the low scoring cards show only a stylized plant;
b) the intermediate card also shows a "tanzaku"—a piece of paper traditionally used for writing poetry;
c) the high scoring card shows an animal or object in addition to the plant.

January: pine

20 points	5 points	1 point	1 point
Pine with crane	Red lettered tanzaku	Plain pine	Plain pine

February: plum

10 points	5 points	1 point	1 point
Plum with nightingale	Red lettered tanzaku	Plain plum	Plain plum

March: cherry

20 points	5 points	1 point	1 point
Cherry with curtain	Red lettered tanzaku	Plain cherry	Plain cherry

April: wisteria

10 points	5 points	1 point	1 point
Wisteria with cuckoo	Plain red tanzaku	Plain wisteria	Plain wisteria

May: iris

10 points	5 points	1 point	1 point
Iris with bridge	Plain red tanzaku	Plain iris	Plain iris

June: peony

10 points	5 points	1 point	1 point
Peony with butterfly	Blue tanzaku	Plain peony	Plain peony

July: clover

10 points
Clover with
wild boar

5 points
Plain red
tanzaku

1 point
Plain clover

1 point
Plain clover

August: pampas

20 points
Pampas with
full moon

10 points
Pampas with
geese

1 point
Plain pampas

1 point
Plain pampas

September: chrysanthemum

10 points
Chrysanthemum
with wine cup

5 points
Blue tanzaku

1 point
Plain
chrysanthemum

1 point
Plain
chrysanthemum

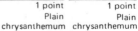

October: maple

10 points
Maple with deer

5 points
Blue tanzaku

1 point
Plain maple

1 point
Plain maple

November: rain (also called willow)

20 points
Rain with poet

10 points
Rain with swallow

5 points
Plain red tanzaku

1 point
Rain and lightning

December: paulownia

20 points
Paulownia with phoenix

1 point
Plain paulownia

1 point
Plain paulownia

1 point
Plain paulownia

Matching flowers : turn of play

a

b

c

GENERAL RULES

Many hanafuda card games share the same general playing arrangements.

Series of games A complete series consists of 12 hands.

The objective is to make the highest total score.

Players Two to seven players may take part in a game, but only two or three can actually play in any hand. (Two-play is not very satisfactory in many hanafuda games.) If there are four to seven players, some must drop out from each hand (see the section on dropping out).

Seating order for all players is decided before the series begins.

Any player deals a single card face up to each player, and the player who receives the card representing the earliest month of the year becomes dealer for the first hand. This player sits where he chooses. The other players take the other seats in counterclockwise rotation, beginning with the player with the next earliest month, who sits to the dealer's right.

If two or more players hold cards of the same month, they are dealt further cards until the tie is settled.

These relative seating positions hold good for the series—even though in each hand only three players will be active.

Shuffle and cut Counting the dealer as first player and going counterclockwise, the third player shuffles and the second player cuts.

Because of the thickness and stiffness of hanafuda cards, shuffling consists of multiple rapid cuts.

Normal rotation of play begins with the player to the dealer's right and goes counterclockwise.

Deal for up to five players

1) The dealer gives each player four cards together, face down, in normal rotation, finishing with himself.

2) He next deals three cards face up into the center of the playing area.

3) He then gives each player three more cards together, face down, in normal rotation, finishing with himself.

4) He finally deals three more cards face up into the center of the playing area—these cards complete the "board."

5) The remainder of the deck is placed face down in the center of the playing area. These cards form the stock, from which players draw cards during the course of play. Any mistake is judged a misdeal, after which the cards are reshuffled, recut, and redealt.

Players may not look at their cards until the deal is completed.

Dealer's hand exchange
can be called by any player
before anyone has looked at
his cards. The player who calls
then exchanges his cards for
those in front of the dealer.
Any number of such
exchanges is permitted.
Dropping out Each player
examines his cards to see
whether he wishes to play the
hand.
The dealer is the first person to
state whether he is playing or
dropping out.
Then the other players state
their intention in normal
rotation. As soon as three
persons have declared to
play, the others drop out
unless any of them feels that
he has a particularly good
hand. In the latter case, a
player may pay a number of
points to the dealer and play
in his place.
When a player drops out, he
places his cards face down on
top of the stock.
It is sometimes ruled that at
least three players must stay
in a hand, in which case the
last players to declare have no
choice if they are needed to

make up the number.
Otherwise it is ruled that if
every player but one drops
out, that player immediately
claims a number of points
from each other player and
then the hand ends.
When the dealer drops out, the
role passes for that hand to the
first player in normal rotation
who has stayed in.

Deal with six players The
deal uses up the entire deck—
there is no stock until one of
the players discards his hand.
Deal with seven players
The blank card is included in
the deck for the deal.
The dealer does not deal any
board cards into the center,
but gives seven cards to each
player in the usual way. This
uses up the entire deck.
The player receiving the blank
card as one of his cards is
obliged to drop out. The blank
card is put out of play and his
remaining six cards become
the board cards.
There is no stock until the
first player who voluntarily
drops out has discarded his
hand.

MATCHING FLOWERS

This is a good family game for young and old. Because it is simple, it is also known as fool flowers. It does, however, make a good introduction to hanafuda play since it illustrates the basic procedures.

The objective A player aims to take cards from the board by matching them with cards from the same suit in his hand. Points are scored according to the point values of the cards matched; and bonus points are scored if the player builds up certain sets among his matched cards.

Play Going to the right from the dealer, play begins with the first player who has stayed in the hand. It continues in normal rotation.

Turn of play

To begin his turn a player examines his cards to see if he has a card of the same month as any of the cards on the board (**a**).

If he has, he exposes the relevant card from his hand and takes the appropriate card from the board. The two cards are placed together face up in front of the player (**b**).

If he is unable to match any card in the board, he must discard any one card from his hand and place it face up as one of the board cards.

In either case, the player then draws one card from the top of the stock and exposes it.

If the drawn card matches the suit of any one of the board cards, the player may take this card and place it and the drawn card face up together in front of him.

If the drawn card does not match any board card it is added to the board (**c**).

The player's turn now ends: a player is only permitted to match from his hand once and to make one draw in any one turn

No board cards If there are no board cards at any time, a player must discard to the board and then draw.

The drawn card can take the discard as usual if they are of the same suit.

No stock If the stock is exhausted play still continues if players have unmatched cards.

In each turn a player must match a card in the board; or, if he cannot match, he must discard any card from his hand to the board.

Three of a kind If three cards of the same suit appear in the board at the beginning of play, then the player who receives the remaining card of that suit may take all three. It does not matter whether he receives the other card in the original deal or by drawing.

If the three board cards are not claimed immediately, they are stacked together until a player claims them.

Tactics of play include, of course, trying to prevent other players from scoring points as well as trying to score points for oneself.

A hand ends when players have no unmatched hand cards remaining.

One player may continue to play even after all the others have finished.

Scoring A player's score for a hand is made up of basic points and bonus points.

1) Basic points: each player receives the points total of the cards that he has matched.

2) Bonus points are scored for combinations formed from any of a player's matched cards. One card may be reckoned in any number of combinations. Standard combinations are shown in the table.

Continuing play The series continues with the next hand. The player with the highest points total from a hand becomes the dealer for the next hand.

"Low man out" Any player who is dealt a very poor hand can request a hand of low man out. He then tries to make as few points as possible—but he must always make a match if he can.

If, at the end of the hand, he has fewer than 20 points, then the winner of the hand loses all his points for that hand. Other players score normally.

Result The winner is the player who makes the highest total score over the series.

Bonus combinations at "matching flowers"

Name	Number of cards	Point score	Cards needed
Straight paulownia	4	10	All cards of paulownia suit
Straight wisteria	4	10	All cards of wisteria suit
Grass tanzaku	3	20	Wisteria, iris, clover tanzaku cards
Boar-deer-a-butterfly	3	20	Clover-and-boar, maple-and-deer, peony-and-butterfly
Crane-phoenix-moon	3	20	Pine-and-crane, paulownia-and-phoenix, pampas-and-full moon
Three bright	3	30	Pine-and-crane, plum-and-nightingale, cherry-and-curtain
Six tanzaku	6	30	Any six tanzaku cards, except the rain tanzaku
The views	2 or 3	20 for 2 / 40 for 3	Pampas-and-full moon, chrysanthemum-and-wine cup, cherry-and-curtain cards
Blue tanzaku	3	40	Peony, chrysanthemum, maple tanzaku cards
Red lettered tanzaku	3	40	Pine, plum, cherry tanzaku cards
Seven tanzaku	7	40	Any seven tanzaku cards, except the rain tanzaku
Four bright	4	60	Pine-and-crane, cherry-and-curtain, pampas-and-full moon, paulownia-and-phoenix cards
Five bright	5	100	"Four bright" and rain-and-poet card
Straight rain	4	10*	All cards of rain suit

*But also all bonus points of all other players for that hand are lost

Bonus score combinations (examples)

The views

Boar—deer—butterfly

(Word Games next page)

Word
Games

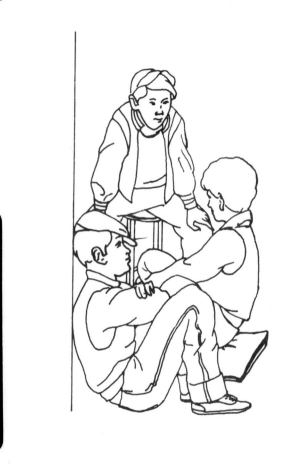

Word games

Play with words is a popular form of amusement, newly devised games taking their place alongside old favorites. Word games range from straightforward spelling games to more complex games requiring verbal dexterity or skillful guesswork. Most of the games can be played by any number of people.

STANDARD SPELLING BEE

One person is chosen as leader, and the other players sit facing him.

The leader is either given a previously prepared list of words or he makes one up himself. It is a good idea to have a dictionary to hand in case of disputes.

Play The leader reads out the first word on his list and the first player tries to spell it. He is allowed ten seconds in which to make an attempt at the correct spelling.

If he succeeds, he scores one point and the next word is read out for the next player. If he makes a mistake, the leader reads out the correct spelling. The player does not score for that word, and the next word is read out for the next player. (Alternatively, the player is eliminated from the game for an incorrect answer.) Play continues around the group of players until all the words on the list have been spelled.

The winner is the player with the most points at the end of the game.

GREEDY SPELLING BEE

In this version of standard spelling bee, if a player spells a word correctly he is given another word to spell. Only when he makes a mistake does the next player take a turn— and he starts with the incorrectly spelled word.

One point is scored for each correct spelling, and the player with the highest score at the end of the game wins.

BACKWARD SPELLING BEE

In this more difficult version of the standard game, players must spell their words backward.

Scoring is the same as in standard spelling bee.

RIGHT OR WRONG SPELLING BEE

The players should form two teams of equal size, and get in line opposite each other.

The leader calls out a word to each player in turn, alternating between teams. Each time a player spells a word, the player standing opposite him must call out "Right" or "Wrong." If he calls a correctly spelled word wrong or a misspelled word right, he is eliminated from the game and must leave the line. (Players may move around once their numbers have been depleted, so that there is a caller for each player in the other team.)

If the caller makes a correct call, he gets the next word to spell.

The last team to retain any players wins the game.

GRAB ON BEHIND

Also called last and first or alpha and omega, this is another good game for a lot of players.

Players decide on a specific category, such as flowers, cities, or insects.

The first player calls out a word in the chosen category. The next player then follows with another word in the category—but it must begin with the last letter of the previous word. Play continues in this way around the group. For example, if the category were flowers the words might be: mimosa, anemone, edelweiss, sweet pea, and so on.

Players have only five seconds in which to think of a word and may not repeat a word that has already been called.

Anyone failing to think of a word or calling an incorrect word drops out of that round. The last player to stay in wins.

GHOSTS

Ghosts needs concentration and a good vocabulary to win.

The players sit round in a circle and take it in turns to contribute a letter to an unstated word. They try to keep the word going for as long as possible—any player who completes a word loses one of his three "lives."

For example, the first player thinks of any word (about) and calls out its first letter (A). The second player thinks of a word with more than three letters starting with the letter called (agree) and calls out its second letter (G). The third player thinks of a word that begins with AG (agate) and calls out its third letter (A). The next player, thinking of "again," calls out "I."

The fifth player, unable to think of anything other than "again" is forced to add N and thus complete a word. He may also try to bluff his way out of the situation by calling out a letter of an imaginary word, in the hope that none of the others will notice—if they do notice, they may challenge him.

Challenging If a player hesitates for too long or the other players suspect that he has no particular word in mind they may challenge him. The challenged player must state his word, and if he cannot do so he loses a "life."

If his explanation is satisfactory, however, the challenger loses a life.

Scoring Whenever a player completes a word he loses a life and becomes "a third of a ghost." Losing a second life makes him "two-thirds of a ghost," and if he loses a third life he becomes a whole ghost and must drop out of the game.

The player who survives until the end is the winner. (For a longer game, the number of lives may be increased to four or five.)

I-SPY

I-spy is an excellent game for children learning to spell. It is also fun for older children, who can try and outwit each other by "spying" (seeing) inconspicuous objects.

Objective Each player tries to be the first to guess which visible object one of them has spied.

Play Two or more people can play, and one of them is chosen to start.

He says "I spy, with my little eye, something beginning with . . ." and gives the first letter of an object that he has secretly chosen, that must be visible to all the players. (They may have to turn their heads in order to see the object, but they should not need to move about.)

For example, if he chose a vase, he would give the letter V or, if he chose a two-word object, the first letter of each word (eg PF for picture frame).

If the player chooses an object, such as a chair, of which there may be more than one in the room, the other players must guess the particular chair he has in mind.

The game ends as soon as someone has spotted the object that was chosen—he may then spy the next object.

Variation I-spy may be played by very young children if colors rather than first letters are given.

For example, a player may say "I spy, with my little eye, something red" and the others then look for the red object that he has in mind.

INITIAL LETTERS

The players sit in a circle. One of them puts a question—it may be as farfetched as he likes—to the others. Each of them in turn must reply with a two-word answer, beginning with the initials of his or her name. Players have only five seconds in which to think of an answer.

For example, if the question were "What is your favorite food?" Bruce Robertson could reply "Boiled rice," and Robert Chapman might say "Roquefort cheese."

When all the players have answered, the second player asks a question.

Any player who fails to answer after five seconds or who gives a wrong answer drops out of the game; the winner is the last person to stay in.

INITIAL ANSWERS

This is a good game for a large group of people. The players sit in a circle and one of them starts by thinking of any letter of the alphabet (eg S). He must then think of a three-letter word beginning with that letter and give a definition of his word, for example "S plus two letters is a father's child."

The second person in the circle has to try and guess the word ("son"), and he then thinks of a word of four letters also beginning with S. He might choose "soup" and define it as "S plus three letters makes a tasty start to a meal" for the person sitting next to him to guess.

This next person, after guessing the word correctly, must think of a five-letter word—perhaps "snail"—defining it as "S plus four letters carries a house on its back."

The game continues in this way, with each person having to think of a word beginning with the chosen letter, and each word having one letter more than the previous word. Any player who fails to think of an appropriate word, or who fails to guess a word must drop out.

The last person left in the game is the winner.

A different letter of the alphabet should be chosen for the next round.

TRAVELER'S ALPHABET

In this game, the first player says "I am going on a journey to Amsterdam," or any other town or country beginning with A.

The next person then asks "What will you do there?" The verb, adjective, and noun used in the answer must all begin with A; for example, "I shall acquire attractive antiques."

The second player must then give a place name and an answer using the letter B, the third player uses the letter C, and so on around the players. Any player who cannot respond is eliminated from the game.

If the players wish to make the game more taxing, they may have to give an answer that is linked with the place they have chosen. For example, a player might say "I am going to Greece to guzzle gorgeous grapes."

If a player gives an inappropriate answer he may be challenged by another player. If that player cannot think of a more fitting sentence, the first player may stay in the game. Should the challenger's sentence be

suitably linked, the first player is eliminated.

BUZZ

This game should be played as briskly as possible for maximum enjoyment.

The players sit in a circle. One player calls out "One," the next player "Two," the next "Three," and so on.

As soon as the number five, or any multiple thereof, is reached, the players must say "Buzz." If the number contains a five but is not a multiple of five, only part of it is replaced by buzz. (For example, 52 would be "buzz two.")

If a player forgets to say buzz or hesitates too long, he drops out; the last player to stay in the game is the winner.

FIZZ

This is played exactly like buzz, except that players say "Fizz" for sevens or multiples of seven.

BUZZ-FIZZ

Buzz-fizz combines the two games, so that 57, for example, becomes buzz-fizz.

I LOVE MY LOVE

In I love my love, players have to think of an adjective beginning with each letter of the alphabet to complete a given statement.

The first player starts by saying "I love my love because she is . . ." using any adjective beginning with A. The next person repeats the phrase, but his adjective must begin with B, the next person's with C, and so on through the alphabet.

Alternatively, each player must say a different refrain, as well as using an adjective with a different letter. The refrains may be:

"Her name is . . . ;
She lives in . . . ;
And I shall give her . . ."

Players may write down the refrains decided upon if they wish, but there must be no hesitation over the answers. Any player who hesitates or gives an incorrect answer drops out of the game, and the winner is the last person left in.

A WAS AN APPLE PIE

This is a similar game to I love my love, but players must think of a verb instead of an adjective.

The first player says: "A was an apple pie, A ate it," and other players might add "B baked it," "C chose it," "D dropped it," and so on.

TABOO

In taboo—sometimes called never say it—players try to avoid saying a particular letter of the alphabet.

One player is the questioner and chooses which letter is to be "taboo."

He then asks each of the players in turn any question he likes. The respondent must answer with a sensible phrase or sentence that does not contain the forbidden letter—if he does use the taboo letter, he is out.

The last player to stay in the game wins and becomes the next questioner.

I—spy

JOIN THE CLUB

This game needs players who have not played it before. Only when they guess a secret solution, known only to the leader, are they allowed to "join the club."

The leader says: "Mrs Pettigrew doesn't like tea, what does she like?"

The other players suggest different things and the leader tells them whether they are right or wrong—if they are wrong they must drop out. Play continues until all the players have dropped out, or until one of them guesses the solution: "tea" is really the letter T, so that any answer given should not contain it. For example, answers like "chocolate," "tomatoes," or "tequila" would eliminate a player.

If a player guesses the solution, the leader says "Join the club!"

Other questions the leader could ask are:

"Our cook doesn't like peas, what does he prefer?"; or "The G-man never takes his ease, what does he take?"

COFFEEPOT

Coffeepot is a word substitution game that is easily learned and a lot of fun.

The objective is for one player to guess an activity chosen by the other players. He does so by asking questions in which he substitutes the word "coffeepot" for the unknown word.

Play One player leaves the room while the others choose a verb or participle describing an activity—for instance "laugh" and "eat" or "laughing" and "eating." The player then returns to the room and puts a question to each of the players in turn, saying something like "Do you often coffeepot?" The players must answer truthfully, with either a straight "Yes" or "No," or with answers like "Only sometimes" or "When it rains."

As the guesser does not know what the activity is, some of the questions will be hilarious —which is where the fun of the game lies.

If he manages to guess the word, the player whose answer enabled him to do so becomes the next guesser. If he cannot guess the word within a reasonable time, he must take another turn at guessing.

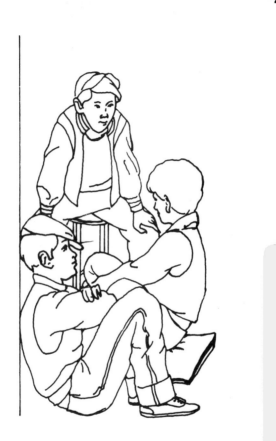

TEAKETTLE (TEAPOT)

As in coffeepot, one of the players leaves the room while the others think of a word for him to guess.

The choice of word might be quite tricky, as it must be one with several meanings. Examples are: rain, reign, rein; or way, weigh, whey.

The player comes back into the room and listens to the others as they make conversation; he may join in if he likes. Sentences must have "teakettle" in place of the chosen word, so that a player might say: "It always seems to teakettle(rain) when I take my baby for a walk."

As soon as he guesses the word, another player takes a turn at guessing a new word.

A variation of teakettle is for the first player to select the word, and the other players to guess what it is as he makes up different sentences. The first person to guess the word correctly may then take a turn at choosing a word.

ASSOCIATIONS

Associations needs quick thinking, as the slightest hesitation eliminates a player from the game!

One person starts by saying any word (preferably a noun). As quickly as possible, the player next to him says the first word that the first player's word brought to mind, and so on around the group, beginning again with the first player.

If a player hesitates before saying a word, he drops out—if he manages to stay in the game longer than all the other players, he wins.

ASSOCIATION CHAIN

This game can be played as a continuation of the last game. As soon as the chain has been formed, the last player to have called out a word starts to repeat the chain backward. If he makes a mistake, he drops out, and the player before him continues to unravel the chain. This goes on until either the first word is reached, or only one player is left.

The more obvious or striking the associations, the easier it is to unravel the chain.

NUMBER ASSOCIATIONS

Number associations needs a person to call out any number between 1 and 12.

As soon as he has said a number, the players call out an appropriate association. For example, if the number called is seven, a player could call "Deadly sins."

The first player to call out a correct association scores one point. Other players may challenge a reply if they feel it is inappropriate. If the leader agrees with the challenge, that player loses one point from his score.

An association may not be repeated.

At the end of the game, the winner is the person with the highest number of points.

I WENT ON A TRIP

Each player tries to remember and repeat a growing list of items.

One of the players chooses any article he likes—for example an umbrella—and says "I went on a trip and took my umbrella."

The next player repeats that sentence and adds a second item after "umbrella." In this way the players gradually build up a list of articles.

Each time his turn comes, a player repeats the list and adds another item. Whenever a player cannot repeat the list correctly, the list is closed and the next player in the group begins a new list.

CITY OF BOSTON

City of Boston is very similar to I went on a trip, but the additions are made at the beginning of the sentence. Thus the first player might say "I shall sell you a nosegay of violets when you come to the City of Boston," and each of the other players repeats that sentence, adding an item he will "sell" to the list.

ONE MINUTE PLEASE

One minute please calls for quick wits and imagination as players try to speak for one minute on a given topic.

One player is chosen as timekeeper, and also picks a topic for each player to talk about.

When it is his turn to speak, the player is told his topic. This may be anything from a serious topic such as "The current political situation" to something frivolous like "Why women wear hats."

The player may choose to treat the subject in any manner he pleases and what he says may be utter nonsense, provided he does not deviate from the topic, hesitate unduly, or repeat himself.

Other players may challenge the speaker if they feel he has broken a ruling. If the timekeeper agrees, then that player must drop out and the next player is given his topic. The winner is the player who manages to speak for an entire minute. If two or more players achieve this, the others decide which of the speeches was the best, or alternatively further rounds may be played.

WHAT IS MY THOUGHT

LIKE ? This is a game for those with a lively imagination and the ability to bluff.

Any number of players may take part. One of them thinks of a thing or a person and asks the other players "What is my thought like ?"

Each of them then makes a totally random guess (as no clues have been given) as to the object thought of.

Once all the players have made their guesses, they are told the object and are given a moment or two in which to think of a way of justifying the relationship between the object and their own guesses. For example, if the object were a tiger and the first player had suggested a fire engine, he might legitimately explain "A fire engine is like a tiger because they both roar down the road!"

As some of the explanations may be rather farfetched they may be discussed among the other players. Any player whose explanation is disallowed must pay a forfeit. If all the players give satisfactory answers, the questioner must pay a forfeit. A different questioner is chosen for each subsequent round.

WHO AM I?

This is a fairly simple game, in which one player does all the guessing.

He leaves the room while the other players think of any well-known personality—real or fictional, dead or alive. The guesser returns to the room and asks "Who am I?" The other players each reply with a clue to the character's identity.

If the character is Napoleon, for example, answers given might be:

"You are rather short and stout;"

"You are a great strategist at war;"

"You underestimated the Russian winter."

When each of the players has given a reply, the guesser may make three guesses as to the identity of the person.

If he fails to guess correctly, he is told the answer.

Another player is always chosen for the next round.

PROVERBS

In this guessing game, one player has to discover a proverb hidden in the other players' answers to his questions. (It is sometimes called hidden proverbs, or guessing proverbs.)

While he is out of the room the other players select a proverb. He returns to the room and asks each player in turn a question—it may be about anything at all, such as "What did you have for breakfast today?"

Each answer must contain one word from the proverb in the correct order. As soon as all the words have been used up, the players begin again with the first word of the proverb. The questioner may make as many guesses at the proverb as he likes within a time limit of, say, ten minutes. If he cannot guess the proverb, he is told the answer and another player takes over as guesser in the next round.

BOTTICELLI

This is another game featuring famous people, and requires a good general knowledge.

One person chooses a personality, and tells the other players the initial of his surname. For example, he might say "M" for Groucho Marx.

Taking turns, each player must think of a character whose name begins with that letter, and give a description of him without naming the person he has in mind. If he thought of Mickey Mouse, he would ask

"Are you a Walt Disney cartoon character?"
If the first player recognizes the description, he answers "No, I am not Mickey Mouse," and another player may make a guess.
If the first player does not recognize the description, however, the player who gave it may then ask a direct question that will give him and the other players a lead, such as "Are you in the entertainment business?" The first player must give a truthful "Yes" or "No" reply.
The first person to guess the personality wins the round and may choose the next character.
If nobody succeeds in guessing the personality after a reasonable length of time, the first player tells them the answer and may choose again for the new round.

ANIMAL, VEGETABLE, OR MINERAL

Sometimes called twenty questions, this game is one of the oldest and most familiar word guessing games. It may be made as simple or as difficult as the players wish, and can provide plenty of scope for intellectual dexterity as the players try to guess an object thought of by one of the others.
Players The game needs two or more players, or two teams. It is often helpful to have a non-playing person to act as referee.
Play One of the players thinks of an object. It may be

general (eg "a ship"), specific (eg "the *Lusitania*"), or a feature (eg "the bridge of the *Lusitania*").
Sometimes the player then tells the others the composition of his chosen object (ie animal, vegetable, or mineral)—in an alternative version the players must guess it themselves.
The three categories may be defined as follows:
1) animal: all forms of animal life or anything of animal origin, eg a centipede, a tortoiseshell comb;
2) vegetable: all forms of vegetable life or anything of vegetable origin, eg flax, a wooden mallet;
3) mineral: anything inorganic or of inorganic origin, eg soda water, a mirror.
Objects are often a combination of categories, for example a can of beer or a leather shoe. (The referee may be consulted if the player is unsure as to the category of an object.)
The player usually indicates the number of words in the object—excluding the definite or indefinite article. The other players can ask anything up to 20 questions to try to guess the object. They should ask questions of a general nature rather than make random guesses, until they feel confident that they are near to knowing the object. As each question is put to the player, he must reply either "Yes," "No," or "I don't know" as appropriate. In one version of the game, he may be

allowed to qualify his answer if necessary by saying, for example, "Yes, in certain conditions."

The referee may intervene if he feels the player has given a wrong or misleading answer; he may also be consulted for guidance on a particular point.

End The first player to guess the object correctly may choose an object for a new round of play.

If no one has guessed the object by the time 20 questions have been asked (usually the referee keeps a count) the players are told what it was, and the same person may choose an object for the next round, or—if two teams are playing—a person in the other team may choose.

MAN AND OBJECT

In man and object, a player thinks of a person and something identified with him.

The person may be someone known personally to all the players, or a famous personality or fictional character. Examples might be an eskimo and his igloo, or Dante and the Inferno.

Playing procedure is the same as for animal, vegetable, or mineral—except that the players may be allowed to ask more than 20 questions.

(Pencil & Paper Games next page)

Pencil and paper games

Pencil and paper games need only the simplest equipment, yet they can provide great scope for the imagination, increase a player's general knowledge, and—above all—be a highly enjoyable way of passing time. Pencil and paper games fall basically into two categories: word games and games in which pictures or symbols are drawn.

KEYWORD

Keyword, sometimes called hidden words, can be played by any number of people. The players choose a "keyword" containing at least seven letters. Each player then tries to make as many words as possible from the letters in the keyword. The letters may be used in any order, but a letter may be used in any one word only as many times as it appears in the keyword. Generally, proper nouns (capitalized words) or words with fewer than four letters are not allowed; nor are abbreviations or plurals. The game may be played just for interest, with players working together; or it may be made into a contest, with individuals competing to find most words in an agreed length of time.

JUMBLED WORDS (ANAGRAMS)

Any number of players may take part. One of them prepares a list of words belonging to a particular category (eg flowers, cities, poets) and jumbles up the letters in each word. Each of the other players is given a list of the jumbled words and their category, and tries to rearrange the letters back into the original words. For example, "peilmidhun" should be "delphinium" and "wodronsp" should be "snowdrop." The first player to rearrange all the words correctly, or the player with most correct words after a given time, wins the game. More experienced players may like to make up anagrams of their own by rearranging the letters in a word to make one or more other words, eg "angered" is an anagram of "derange."

ACROSTICS

Acrostics is another word-building game. A word of at least three letters is chosen. Each player writes the word in a column down the left-hand side of a sheet of paper; he then writes the same word, but with the letters reversed, down the right-hand side of the page.

The player fills in the space between the two columns with the same number of words as there are letters in the keyword—and starting and ending each word with the letter at either side.

For example, if the keyword is "stem," a player's words might read: scream, trundle, earliest, manageress.

The winner may be either the first person to fill in all the words, or the player with the longest or most original words.

TRANSFORMATION

Two words with the same number of letters are chosen. Each player writes down the two words. He tries to change the first word into the second word by altering only one letter at a time, and each time forming a new word.

For example, "dog" could be changed to "cat" in four words as follows: dog, cog, cot, cat. It is easiest to begin with three or four letter words until the players are quite practiced—when five or even six letter words may be tried.

The winner is the player who completes the changes using the fewest number of words.

FILL INS

A list of 30 to 40 words is prepared and kept hidden from the players.

Each player is then given the first and last letters and the number of letters missing from each word on the list.

The winner is the first player to fill in all the blanks correctly. Alternatively, the players may be allowed an agreed length of time and then the winner is the player with the most correct words.

DOG
COG
COT
CAT

CATEGORIES

Perhaps one of the best-known pencil and paper games, categories can be played at either a simple or a sophisticated level.

Preparation Each player (there may be any number) is given a pencil and a piece of paper.

The players decide on between six and a dozen different categories; these may be easy ones for children (eg girls' or boys' names, animals, colors) or more difficult for adults (eg politicians, rivers, chemicals). Each player lists the categories on his piece of paper.

One of the players chooses any letter of the alphabet—preferably an "easy" letter such as "a" or "d" if children are playing. Experienced players can make the game more challenging by choosing more difficult letters such as "j" or "k."

Players may decide to play to an agreed time limit of say 15 minutes.

Play The players try to find a word beginning with the chosen letter for each of the categories (eg if the chosen letter is "p" all the words must begin with that letter). They write down their words next to the appropriate category.

The more unusual or original the word, the better—thus even if simple categories have been chosen, there is still plenty of scope for ingenuity.

Scoring Writing must stop as soon as the time limit is up, or as soon as one player has finished.

Each player in turn then reads out his list of words. If he has found a word not thought of by any of the other players, he scores two points for that word. If, however, one or more of the other players has also chosen the same word, each of them scores only one point. If the player could not find a word at all, or if his choice of word did not correctly fit the category, he gets no points. (Any disagreement about the relevance of a word to a category must be solved by a vote among the other players.) The winner is the player with the highest score for his list of words.

Subsequent rounds Any number of rounds may be played, using either the same or different categories; the chosen letter, however, must be different for each round. Players may take it in turns to choose a letter at the start of a round.

Players make a note of their scores at the end of each round. The winner is the player with the highest points total at the end of the final round.

GUGGENHEIM

Guggenheim is a slightly more complicated version of categories. Instead of choosing only one letter for each round of play, the players choose a keyword of about four or five letters. The letters of the keyword are written spaced out to the right of the list of categories, and players try to find words for each of the categories beginning with the letter heading each column.

CROSSWORDS

This intriguing game can be adapted for play by any number of people.

If up to five people are playing, each of them draws a square divided into five squares by five on a sheet of paper.

If more people take part, or if players wish to lengthen the game, the number of squares can be increased to, say, seven by seven.

Each of the players in turn calls out any letter of the alphabet. As each letter is called, all players write it into any square of their choice, with the objective of forming words of two or more letters reading either across or down.

Generally, abbreviations or proper nouns (names, etc) may not be used.

Once a letter has been written down, it cannot be moved to another square.

Players continue to call out letters until all the individual squares have been filled.

The number of points scored is equal to the number of letters in each word (one-letter words do not count). Thus a three-letter word scores three points. If a word fills an entire row or column, one bonus point is scored in addition to the score for that word.

No ending of a word can form the beginning of another word in the same row or column. For example, if a row contains the letters "i, f, e, n, d" the player may score four points for the word "fend" but cannot in addition score two points for the word "if."

Each player adds together each of his horizontal and vertical totals; the winning player is the one with the highest score.

SYNONYMS

A list of 10 to 20 words is prepared, and a copy given to each player.

The objective is to find a synonym (word with the same meaning) for each word on the list. If a player can think of more than one synonym for any word he should write down the shortest one.

After an agreed length of time, the players' lists are checked.

The winner is the player who finds a synonym for the most words, or, if two or more players have an equal number of synonyms, the player with the lowest total of letters in his synonyms.

GEOGRAPHY RACE

This is an ideal game for a large group of players, and a good way of brushing up one's knowledge of geography!

The players are formed into two teams, and one person acts as umpire. If possible, the teams should sit in parallel rows. The first person in each team is given a piece of paper and something to write with.

The object of the game is for each person in a team to write down the name of a town or city that lies in a specified direction of the last town on the list.

Play The umpire chooses the name of any well-known town or city and specifies in which compass direction the other towns must lie.

For example, he might say "Towns to the east of Berlin." He gives a start signal, and the first person in each team must write down a town that lies to the east of Berlin.

The player then hands the pencil and paper to the next person in his team, who writes down a town to the east of the town chosen by the first player.

Play continues in this way until the last member in the team has written down a town.

Scoring As soon as one team has finished, the umpire checks both teams' answers. The team that finished first scores a bonus of five points. In addition, each correct answer scores one point, and one point is deducted for each incorrect answer.

The team with the highest number of points after one or more rounds wins.

TELEGRAMS

Players are given a list of 15 letters, and must use each of them—in the order given—as the initial letter of a word in a 15-word telegram.

(Alternatively, the players are given a word of about 10–15 letters, eg blackberries, so that the first word must begin with "b," the second with "l," and so on.)

The telegram may include one or two place names and may— if the player wishes—have the name of the "sender" as the last word.

Stops (or periods) may be used for punctuation.

The winner is the first player to complete his telegram, or, if a time limit has been set, the player whose telegram is judged to be the best at the end of the time set.

S CREA **M**
T RUNDLE **E**
E ARLIES **T**
M ANAGERES **S**

Categories	Letters P.	S.
Composer	Faderewski	Strauss
City	Port o' Spain	Sydney
Mountain	Pilatus	Stromboli
Girl's Name	Phyllis	Sarah

Categories	G	A	M	E
Composer	Grieg	Albinoni	Mozart	Elgar
City	Georgetown	Amsterdam	Mombassa	Essen
Mountain	Grossglockner	Anapurna	Matterhorn	Etna
Girl's name	Gertrude	Abigail	Michelle	Elinor

Telegrams

BLACKBERRIES

BRING LAMP AND CHISEL STOP KNOW REST
ENTRY ROUTE STOP REST IS EASY STOP
                                    SID

Crosswords

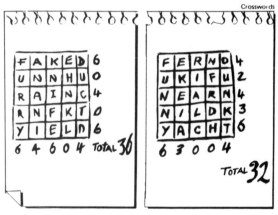

F	A	K	E	D	6
U	N	N	H	U	0
R	A	I	N	C	4
R	N	F	K	T	0
Y	I	E	L	D	6

6 4 6 0 4 TOTAL 30

F	E	R	N	D	4
U	K	I	F	U	2
N	E	A	R	N	4
N	I	L	D	K	3
Y	A	C	H	T	6

6 3 0 0 4

TOTAL 32

Pictures is best played by two teams of at least three players each. In addition, there must be an organizer who belongs to neither team.

The organizer makes a list of half a dozen or so book titles, proverbs, or other subjects (they need not be in the same category).

The organizer whispers the first title on the list to one player from each team. This player returns to his team (the teams should preferably be in separate rooms) and must draw a picture representing the title. He may add to his drawing or make further drawings—until one of his teammates has correctly guessed the answer. (No verbal clues may be given, however!)

As soon as one player has guessed the title, he may go to the organizer for the next title on the list.

The winning team is the first one to guess all the titles on the organizer's list.

HANGMAN

Hangman is a popular game for two or more players. One person thinks of a word of about five or six letters. He writes down the same number of dashes as there are letters in his word.

The other players may then start guessing the letters in the word, calling one letter at a time. If the guess is a successful one, the letter is written by the first player above the appropriate dash— if it appears more than once in a word it must be entered as often as it occurs.

If the guess is an incorrect one, however, the first player may start to draw a hanged man— one line of the drawing representing each wrong letter.

The other players must try to guess the secret word before the first player can complete the drawing of the hanged man.

If one of the players guesses the word (this should become easier as the game progresses) he may take a turn at choosing a word. If the hanged man is completed before the word is guessed, the same player may choose another word.

To make the game more difficult, longer words may be chosen, or even a group of words making a proverb or title of a book or film—the player gives the others a clue as to the category.

Hang-
man

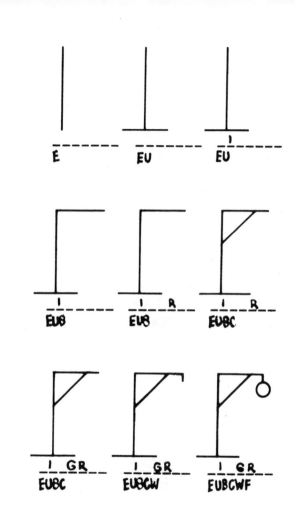

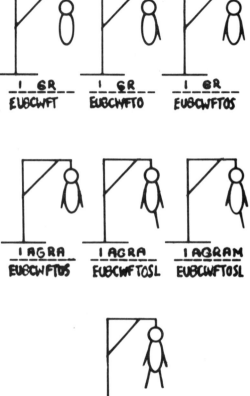

_ I _ GR _ _ _
EUBCWFT

_ I _ GR _ _ _
EUBCWFTO

_ I _ GR _ _ _
EUBCWFTOS

_ I _ AGRA _ _
EUBCWFTOS

_ I _ AGRA _ _
EUBCWFTOSL

_ I _ AGRAM _
EUBCWFTOSL

_ I _ AGRAM _
EUBCWFTOSLP

TICK-TACK-TOE

A favorite for generations, tick-tack-toe (or noughts and crosses) is a game for two people that may be over in a matter of seconds!

Two vertical lines are drawn with two horizontal lines crossing them, forming nine spaces.

Players decide which of them is to draw noughts (circles) and which of them crosses. Taking alternate turns, the players make their mark in any vacant space until one of them manages to get three of his marks in a row (either horizontally, vertically, or diagonally). He then draws a line through his winning row and the game comes to an end. If neither player succeeds in forming a row, the game is considered drawn.

As the player who draws first has a better chance of winning, players usually swap their starting order after each game.

THREE-DIMENSIONAL TICK-TACK-TOE

Based on the standard game, the three-dimensional version offers a lengthier and more challenging alternative. Three-dimensional tick-tack-toe can be bought as a game, but can equally well be played with pencil and paper. The cube may be represented diagrammatically by 64 squares—as shown. For actual play, each "layer" of the cube is drawn out individually.

Playing procedure is similar to standard tick-tack-toe, but the winner is the first player to get four of his marks in a row (see illustrations).

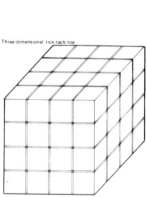

Three-dimensional tick-tack-toe

The cube

Nine winning rows

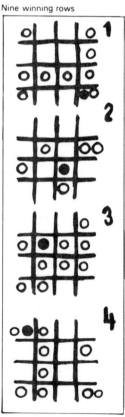

Boxes

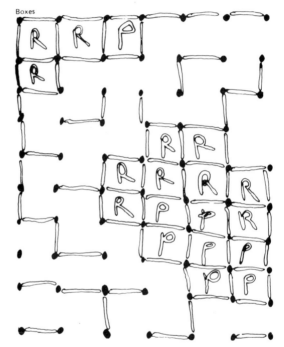

BOXES

This is a simple but amusing game for two players. Any number of dots is drawn on a piece of paper—the dots are drawn in rows to form a square. Ten rows by ten is a good number.

Players take alternate turns. In each turn they may draw a horizontal or vertical line to join up any two dots that are next to each other.

The objective is to complete (with a fourth line) as many squares or "boxes" as possible. Whenever a player completes a box he initials it and may draw another line. He may continue his turn until he draws a line that does not complete a box.

As soon as there are no more dots to be joined—all the boxes having been filled—the game ends. The player with the highest number of initialed boxes is the winner.

Another way of playing is to try to form the lowest number of boxes—the players join up as many lines as they can before being forced to complete a box. The winner is the player with the fewest initialed boxes.

SPROUTS

Sprouts has certain similarities with boxes, but needs rather more ingenuity to win!

Two players take part. About six or so dots are drawn— well spaced out—on a sheet of paper (more may be drawn for a longer game).

Taking alternate turns, each player draws a line joining any two dots or joining a dot to itself. He then draws a dot anywhere along the line he has just made, and his turn ends.

When drawing a line, the following rules must be observed:
1) no line may cross itself or cross a line that has already been drawn;
2) no line may be drawn through a dot;
3) a dot may only have three lines leaving it.

The last person able to draw a legitimate line is the winner.

Sprouts

Disallowed sprouts

CRYSTALS

In this sophisticated pattern visualizing game, each player tries to form symmetrical shapes known as "crystals."

Equipment All that is needed is a sheet of squared (graph) paper and as many differently colored crayons as there are players.

The number of squares used for each game depends on the number of players: if two take part (the best number) about 20 rows of 20 squares each would form a suitable area.

Objective Each player attempts to "grow" crystals on the paper with the aim of filling more squares than his opponent.

A player does not score points for the number of crystals he grows, but for the number of squares his crystals cover.

A crystal is made up of "atoms," each of which occupies a single square. In growing crystals, players must observe certain rules of symmetry that determine whether or not a crystal is legitimate.

The symmetry of a crystal can be determined by visualizing four axes through its center: horizontal, vertical, and two diagonal axes. Once the axes have been "drawn," it should theoretically be possible to fold the crystal along each of the four axes to produce corresponding "mirror" halves that, when folded, exactly overlay each other (ie are the same shape and size).

In addition to the rules of symmetry, players must observe the following:

a) a legitimate crystal may be formed from four or more atoms drawn by one player only;

b) the atoms forming a crystal must be joined along their sides—they may not be connected only by their corners;

c) a crystal may not contain any empty atoms (ie holes).

Play Players decide on their playing order and each one in turn shades in any one square of his choice—each player using a crayon of a different color.

In their first few turns, players rarely try to grow a crystal. Instead, they place single atoms around the playing area in order to establish potential crystal sites. As play progresses, players will see which atoms are best placed for growing crystals and add to them as appropriate.

Crys-
tals

Crystals

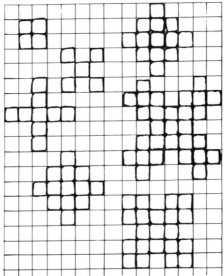

When a player thinks he has grown a crystal, he declares it, and rings the area that it covers.

A player with a winning advantage will try to retain the lead by either blocking his opponents' attempts at growing crystals, or by growing long narrow crystals that—although not high scoring—restrict the playing area.

Play ends when no blank squares are left, or when the players agree that no more crystals can be formed.

Scoring Players work out which of the crystals are legitimate, and count the number of squares each crystal covers.

Any crystal that does not demonstrate symmetry around each of the four axes is not legitimate and does not score. The number of squares in the legitimate crystals that each player has grown are added, and the player with most squares wins the game.

Disallowed

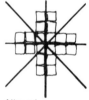

Allowed

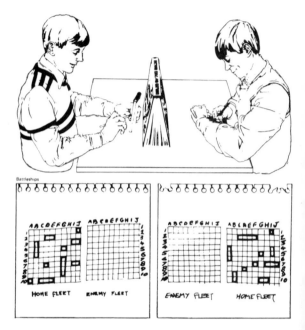

Battleships

HOME FLEET ENEMY FLEET

ENEMY FLEET HOME FLEET

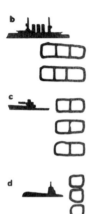

bottom left-hand square is A10, etc). Each player marks one playing area his "home fleet" and the other playing area the "enemy fleet."

Each player has his own fleet of ships that he may position anywhere within his home fleet area.

His fleet comprises:

a) one battleship, four squares long;

b) two cruisers, each three squares long;

c) three destroyers, each two squares long; and

d) four submarines, each one square only.

He "positions" his ships by outlining the appropriate number of squares.

The squares representing each ship must be in a row, either across or down. There must also be at least one vacant square between ships.

The players' objective is to destroy their opponent's entire fleet by a series of "hits." Players take alternate turns. In each turn, a player may attempt three hits: he calls out the names of any three squares—marking them on his enemy fleet area as he does so.

His opponent must then consult his own home fleet area to see whether any of these three squares are occupied. If they are, he must state how many and the category of boat hit.

In order to sink a ship, every one of its component squares must have received a hit. The game continues with both players marking the state of

BATTLESHIPS

This is an extremely popular game for two players, each of whom needs a pencil and a sheet of squared (graph) paper.

The players should sit so that they cannot see each other's papers. Each of them draws two identical playing areas, ten squares by ten squares in size. In order to identify each square, the playing areas have numbers down one side and letters across the top (thus the top left-hand square is A1; the

their own and their enemy's fleets—this may be done by shading or outlining squares, or in some other manner of the players' choice.
There is no limit to the number of hits each player may attempt—the game comes to an end as soon as one player destroys his opponent's fleet.

BURIED TREASURE

This is a very much simpler version of battleships and is particularly suitable for young children. It is a game for two, with a third person needed to help at the beginning of the game.
Each player draws an area nine squares by nine and marks it in the same manner as for battleships, so that each square has a name.
The third person designates any four of the letters from A to I to one player, and any four of the remaining letters to the other player; he then does the same thing with the numbers from 1–9.
Neither player may know which letters and numbers have been designated to his opponent, nor which letter and number are left over—this is the square in which the treasure is "buried" and which the players must try to identify.

Buried treasure

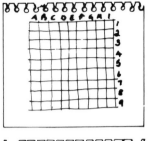

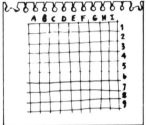

Players take turns to ask each other whether they hold a particular letter or number. Although a respondent must always give a truthful answer, a player may—if he wishes—enquire about a letter or number that he holds himself, so as to mislead his opponent. The first player to locate the treasure by this mixture of bluff and elimination wins the game.

SQUIGGLES

This is a game for two people, each of whom should have a piece of paper, and a pencil different in color from the other player's.

Each player scribbles very quickly on his piece of paper—the more abstract the squiggle, the better.

Players then exchange papers and set themselves a time limit of, for example, two minutes, in which they must use every bit of the squiggle to make a picture. Ingenuity is more important than artistic ability—a third person could be asked to judge which of the players has used his squiggle more inventively.

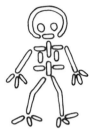

Squiggles

Acting word games

In charades, "the game," dumb crambo, and in the manner of the word, one team mimes a word for the other team to guess. All these games are old favorites requiring only a lively imagination and a little acting ability. Amusement derives not only from the players' acting attempts but also from the often bizarre guesses made by the other team.

CHARADES

Charades is probably the best known and most popular of all acting and guessing games.
The objective is for one team to guess a word with several syllables that is acted out in mime by the other team.
Play The acting team leaves the room and decides on a suitable word. Usually words of three syllables are chosen, but players may choose words of only two syllables or of four or more.
This word is then presented to the other team in mimed scenes representing the different syllables, and then in a final scene representing the whole word.
Usually there is one scene for each syllable, although players may choose to represent two syllables in a single scene. (For example, the word "decorate" could be broken down as "deck-or-rate" or as "decor-ate.")

A member of the acting team must announce the number of scenes before miming begins. The actors usually leave the room between scenes and the guessing team is then free to discuss its ideas.
It is advisable for players to agree on a time limit for guessing words after the final scene.
An example of the sort of word that might be chosen is "nightingale," which was used in a charade scene in the book Vanity Fair by the nineteenth-century English novelist William Thackeray.
Nightingale breaks down into three syllables and could be represented by:
a) a "night" scene with people going to bed or sleeping;
b) an "inn" scene with people drinking and making merry;
c) a "gale" scene with people being blown down a street;
d) a "nightingale" scene with people flapping their arms and imitating bird song.

Char-
ades

Players Acting guessing games can be played by any number of players divided into two teams.

One team chooses a word or phrase according to the rules of the particular game and then the other team attempts to guess it.

The teams change roles whenever a correct guess is made.

Costumes and other props are not necessary for these games but they can add to the players' enjoyment.

CATEGORY CHARADES

This game is played in the same way as standard charades except that teams must choose words that belong to a previously agreed category and there is no miming of the full word. Ideas for categories are:
a) towns (eg, "came-bridge," "prince-ton");
b) people's names (eg, "rob-in," "car-row-line");
c) animals (eg, "lie-on," "buff-a-low");
d) flowers (eg, "snow-drop," "butter-cup").

PROVERB CHARADES

Proverb charades is played in the same way as standard charades except that teams choose a proverb or well-known quotation, which they then act out word by word or in groups of several words. A good proverb for this game would be "a bird in the hand is worth two in the bush."

SPOKEN CHARADES

This game is played in the same way as standard charades except that the actors speak. Instead of miming scenes representing the syllables and then the full word, players must mention them while acting in the different scenes. This game is easier to play than most charades, and for this reason is particularly popular with your children.

THE GAME

This is a fascinating variation of charades. It is called "the game" because its early enthusiasts claimed that it was truly the game of all games. The players are divided into two teams, and each team nominates a different person to be its actor for each round.

Objective Using conventional gestures and free mime, the actor must convey to his teammates a well-known phrase chosen by the opposing team. The teams compete on a time basis.

Categories Phrases for this game must belong to one of a number of categories previously decided by both teams. Typical categories are the title of a book, play, television series, song, or painting, or a quotation, slogan, or proverb.

Play One team chooses a phrase and whispers it to the actor from the other team. The actor then begins miming, and a person appointed as timekeeper makes a note of the time. The actor should use conventional gestures where possible.

His teammates are allowed to speak, and make guesses as the acting proceeds. The actor, however, is only allowed to reply to their guesses with gestures.

If a correct guess is made, the timekeeper records the time and the teams change roles. (It is advisable to have a time limit, after which the teams must change roles even though the phrase has not been guessed.)

Gestures Players may improvise in their miming, but "the game" is characterized by the use of previously agreed gestures.

Firstly the actor indicates the category of the phrase. For example he can mime holding a book (**a**) for a book title.

To indicate the number of words in the phrase the actor then holds up that number of fingers (**b**).

If the actor is going to mime the entire phrase he forms a circle, either with his thumb and forefinger (**c**) or with his arms.

If he wishes to mime only part of the phrase, he indicates a word by tapping the appropriate finger (**d**). He then counts his fingers to show how many letters there are in this word (**e**). If he wishes to use only part of a mimed word, he must make chopping actions to divide the word into syllables.

When his team makes a correct guess, the actor nods his head. If a guess is along the right lines, he beckons; if totally wrong, he makes a brushing away gesture.

Scoring The game is always scored on the basis of the time taken to guess the phrases. There are, however, two different scoring systems:
a) a round is won by the team that guesses its phrase most quickly and a game is won by the team that wins the most rounds;
b) times for the different rounds are added together and the game is won by the team with the shortest total guessing time.

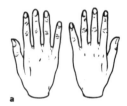

a

b

c

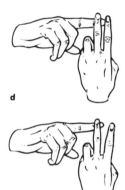

d

e

THE GAME (SIMULTANEOUS)

Some players prefer to have both teams acting the same phrase simultaneously.

In this case it is necessary to appoint a referee, who thinks of a phrase, writes it on two slips of paper, and hands the slips to an actor from each of the teams.

Acting takes place in different rooms—so that players cannot hear the guesses of the opposing team.

A round is won by the team that is first to guess the phrase correctly. A game is won by the team that wins the most rounds.

THE GAME (RELAY)

This is played in the same way as the simultaneous version except that it is organized like a relay race.

The teams must be of equal size and each team member has a turn at being the actor.

As soon as a team guesses a phrase, its next actor goes to the referee, tells him the last phrase, and is given a new one A game is won when a team guesses its last actor's phrase.

DUMB CRAMBO

Dumb crambo is a very old game of the charades family. It was particularly popular in the nineteenth century.

Objective After receiving a rhyming clue, a team attempts to guess and mime a word, usually a verb, chosen by the opposing team.

Play The first team chooses a word, for example "feel," and then tells the second team a word rhyming with it, for example "steal."

It is obviously best for this game to choose a word that has several words rhyming with it. For example, other words that rhyme with "feel" are "heal," "keel," "reel," "deal," and "peel."

The second team then attempts to guess the chosen word and must mime its guesses. A maximum of three guesses is allowed.

If a guess is incorrect, members of the other team hiss or boo; if a guess is correct, they clap their hands.

A team scores one point each time it guesses a word.

Teams change roles after a word is guessed or after three incorrect guesses.

The game is won by the team with most points when play ends.

IN THE MANNER OF THE WORD

This is an amusing acting guessing game in which players attempt to guess adverbs.

Play One player chooses an adverb, such as rapidly, quietly, or amusingly.

The other players, in turn, then ask him to carry out some action "in the manner of the word." For example, a player might say: "eat in the manner of the word," "walk in the manner of the word," or "laugh in the manner of the word."

The player who chooses the adverb must do as the other players ask, and the other players may make guesses as soon as acting begins.

The first player to guess an adverb correctly scores one point. If no one guesses the word after each of the players has asked for an action, the player who chose the adverb receives one point.

The game is won by the player with most points after each of the players has had a turn at choosing an adverb.

Consequences

Consequences is a favorite among children and is a game purely to be enjoyed—there are no winners or losers.
Any number of players can take part, and each of them is provided with a sheet of paper and a pencil.
The objective is to write as many stories as there are participants, with each person contributing to each of the stories.

Play One person is chosen as "caller" (this does not exclude him from taking part). He calls out the first part of the story. Each person writes down an appropriate name, phrase, or sentence, making it as humorous as possible. He then folds over the top of the piece of paper to hide what he has written, and passes the paper to the player to his left.
The caller then says the next part of the story, and the

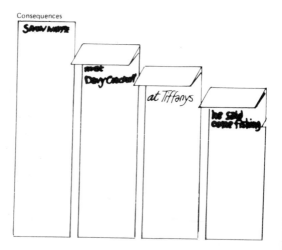

Consequences

Snow White

met Davy Crockett

at Tiffanys

he said come fishing

players write something on the paper they have just received from their neighbors.

This procedure is repeated until the story is complete. Any theme may be used, but the one decribed here is perhaps the best known.

a) "A girl . . ." (players write the name of someone known to them, or alternatively a famous personality or fictional character);

2) "met a boy . . ." (again, the players may choose any name of their choice);

3) "at . . . beside . . . in . . ." (the players may choose any location);

4) "he said . . .";

5) "she said . . .";

6) "the consequence was . . .";

7) "and the world said . . ."

When the story is complete, each player passes the piece of paper on which he wrote the last sentence to the person to his left. The pieces of paper are unfolded and the stories read out one by one—they may not be fictional masterpieces but are sure to provide a lot of fun!

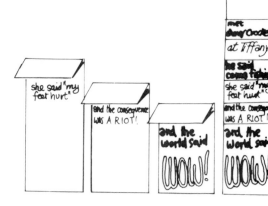

PICTURE CONSEQUENCES

This game follows the same principle as standard consequences, but instead of writing words the players draw parts of the human figure dressed in funny clothing—starting with the head and finishing with the feet.

When the pieces of paper are folded over, a part of the last drawing is left showing, so as to give a lead to the next player. For example, after drawing the head, the paper should be folded so that the edge of the neck is showing. Parts of animals or birds can also be drawn in addition to (or instead of) humans.

After drawing the feet, players may write down the name of the person whom they want the figure to represent!

Picture consequences

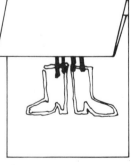

Conse-
quences

Aggression

Aggression is a game in which players fight imaginary battles in a bid to occupy the maximum amount of territory. Two players are ideal—though the game can also be played by three or more, who may choose to form teams. Each player must have a crayon of a different color.

Playing area A large sheet of paper is used. One player begins by drawing the boundaries of an imaginary country; each player in turn then draws the outline of an imaginary country adjoining one or more other countries. Any number of countries may be drawn (20 is an average number if two play) and they can be any shape or size. When the agreed number of countries has been drawn, each is clearly marked with a different letter of the alphabet.

Armies Each player is allotted 100 armies. Taking turns with his opponent, he chooses a country that he intends to occupy and writes within it how many armies he is allocating to it. (Once a country has been occupied, no player may add further armies to it.) This procedure continues until all the countries have been occupied, or until each player has allocated all his armies.

Play The player who chose the first country has the opening move. His objective is to retain more occupied countries than his opponent; to achieve this he "attacks" enemy armies in adjacent countries. (Adjacent countries are defined as those with a common boundary.) A player may attack with armies from more than one country—provided they are all in countries that have a common border with the country under attack.

If the number of armies located in the attacking country or countries is greater than those located in the defending country, the defending army is conquered—its armies are crossed off and can take no further part in the game. (The armies used to conquer a country may be reused.) Players take it in turns to conquer countries until one or both of them cannot mount any further attacks.

Scoring At the end of the game the players total the number of countries each of them retains. The winner is the player with the highest number of unconquered countries— he need not necessarily be the player who made the greatest number of conquests.

Aggression

Drawing
the
boundaries

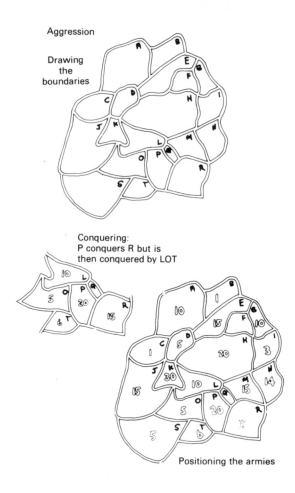

Conquering:
P conquers R but is
then conquered by LOT

Positioning the armies

DRAW THE ELEPHANT'S TAIL

This is similar to the donkey's tail but instead of pinning on a tail players draw one. Each blindfolded player is given a crayon and draws a tail on a picture of an elephant (or any other animal).

CUT-OUT PAIRS

This is a good game for introducing players to each other at the start of a party.

Preparation All sorts of pictures are cut out of magazines, comics, etc. Each picture is pasted onto cardboard and cut into two oddly shaped pieces. (Picture postcards may be used to save time.) There should be one picture for each pair of players.

Play Each player is given one piece of a picture. He then tries to find the player with the other half of the same picture. When two players have a complete picture they write a suitable caption for it. Pictures and captions are displayed and the writers of the funniest caption may win a prize.

MOTHERS AND BABIES

This is another pairing game along the lines of cut-out pairs. For this game players are given a card showing a mother or a baby animal—for example a cow or a calf, a frog or a tadpole. Players then have to find the player with the card showing the other member of their family.

WRONG!

In this game players try to spot deliberate errors in a story that is read to them.

Preparation The organizer writes a short story in which there are numerous errors of fact—for example he might say that he went to the antique shop and bought a new clock.

Play The organizer reads out the story.

If a player spots a mistake he shouts "Wrong!" The first player to call out a mistake scores one point. A player who shouts when there has been no mistake loses one point.

The player with most points at the end of the story wins the game.

MURALS

Preparation The organizer cuts out large pieces of paper for drawing on.

Play Each player in turn is blindfolded, given a crayon, and asked to draw a picture on a piece of paper pinned on the wall.

The subject for the picture is chosen by the other players—good examples are a house, a person, or some kind of animal.

The artist feels the edges of the paper and has one minute in which to draw the chosen subject.

When everyone has had a turn, the drawings can be judged by an adult or by all the players together.

Murals

HAPPY TRAVELERS

Each player tries to be the first to sort the pages of a newspaper into the correct order.

Preparation For each player the pages of a newspaper are put together in the wrong order—some pages may be upside down or back to front —and then folded.

Play Players sit facing each other in two rows. They should sit very close together like passengers on a crowded train.

Each player is given one of the newspapers.

At the word "Go!" each player tries to rearrange the pages of his newspaper into the correct order.

The first player to succeed wins the game.

PRINTERS' ERRORS

In this game players try to set out jumbled lines of a printed article into their correct order.

Preparation A jumbled article is needed for each player. The organizer makes as many copies of the article as he needs and then jumbles each one by cutting it into pieces after each line.

Play Each player is given his jumbled article. When the organizer gives the signal players start to sort out their articles.

The winner is the first player to put his article into the correct order.

SURPRISE SENTENCES

Objective Each team tries to write a sentence, with each player in the team writing one word of it.

Preparation For each team, a large sheet of paper is attached to a wall or to a board propped upright.

Play Each team lines up opposite its sheet of paper and the leader is given a pencil. At the word "Go!" he runs up to his paper and writes any word he likes.

He then runs back to his team, hands the pencil to the next player, and goes to the end of his team.

As soon as the next player gets the pencil, he goes to the paper and adds a second word either in front of, or behind the leader's word. Play continues in this way with each player adding one word. The words should be chosen and put together so that they can be part of a grammatically correct sentence.

Each player, except the last, must avoid completing the sentence. The last player should be able to complete the sentence by adding just one word, and he also puts in the punctuation.

Players may not confer and choose a sentence before writing their words.

End The first team to construct a sentence with one word from each player wins the game.

FRUIT COLORS

Objective Each team tries to be the first to color in pictures of fruit.

Preparation For each team, outlines of fruit (one per player) are drawn on a large sheet of paper. The drawings should be the same for each team.

The sheets of paper are attached to a wall or laid out on a table.

Play Teams line up behind their leaders at the opposite end of the room to the drawings.

Each leader is given a box of crayons.

At the word "Go!" he runs to his team's sheet of paper and colors in one of the pieces of fruit.

He then goes back to his team, hands the box of crayons to the next player and stands at the back of his team.

As soon as the second player gets the crayons, he goes and colors in another fruit and so on down the line of players. If a crayon is dropped on the floor, the player with the box must pick it up.

End The first team to color in all its fruit wins.

Lotto

This family game—the forerunner of games like bingo—originated in Italy. Other names by which it is known are housey housey, tombola, and bolito.

Equipment Lotto is played with special rectangular cards divided into either three or five horizontal and nine vertical rows.

Each horizontal row has five numbered and four blank squares in random arrangement. The vertical rows contain, from left to right respectively, numbers selected from 1 to 10, 11 to 20, 21 to 30, and so on up to 90. No number is duplicated on any other card, and no two cards are alike.

Complementary to the cards is a set of 90 small card counters,

numbered from 1 to 90.

Play As many players may take part as there are cards. Each player is given one card—or more than one if there are any left over.

One player (who may take part in the game if he wishes) is the caller. He puts the card counters into a sack or other container and mixes them well. The caller takes out one counter at a time, calls its number, and gives it to whichever player has the card on which the number appears. That player places the counter on the appropriate square.

End As soon as one player has covered all the numbers on his card in this way, he calls out "Lotto!" His card and counters are checked, and if they are correct he wins the game.

PICTURE LOTTO

This is a variation of standard
lotto, using pictures instead of
numbers. It is an excellent
test of recognition for young
children.

The cards used in picture lotto
are usually divided into six or
eight squares, each showing a
different symbol or picture, eg
flowers, animals, or household
objects.

Each picture has a matching
card. At the start of the game
the caller gathers these small
cards together, mixes them
thoroughly, and picks out one
at a time for the players to see.
The player who claims the
small card takes it and covers
the appropriate picture on the
large card with it. As in lotto,
the first player to cover all the
pictures on his card wins the
game.

DO YOUR OWN GAMES

DO YOUR OWN GAMES

DO YOUR OWN GAMES